The B-Savvy Book

Beauty, Brains, Business & Branding

By Trenice Johnson Ezell

Printed in the United States of America by The GreyRaven Publishing Co. Library of Congress Cataloging -in- Publication Data has been applied for ISBN:978-1548148119

Dedications

This masterpiece is dedicated to my parents. First, this book and my love for business would not have been possible without my parents. To my late beloved mother, though your time here on this earth was short, the value that you left me with as a child was worth more than any words in this book. As a child, I watched you and my dad hustle and co-parent to keep us with shelter, food, and made sure we stayed together as a family. Both of you without knowing, gave me my first business lesson, "Believe in yourself first." Mommy, your early departure changed the course of my life. I remember you used to tell me, "Girl you are determined to give me a headache asking 2000 questions." Those questions sparked the fire that I have today. Today, I am DETERMINED. I am determined to pour into my family, give others my knowledge, and leave a legacy that I know both of will be proud of.

Table of Content

The B Book

Beauty, Brains, Business & Beauty

Acknowledgments

To my loves who made this all so worth it Amir (Our Angel), Torri, Makai, Mercedes, Eldon Jr., and Jamilya, you all have given my life so much joy, laughter, and tons of love. To my Mr. who made my heart whole, Eldon, words cannot even describe how much you have loved on my babies and me. You have made this journey special in so many ways, but I cherish all the love, advice, and support you have given me while writing this book. To my siblings Maurice, Reoshard, Tamika, Michelle, Iieshia, Jabar, Robert, Roderick, Felicia, Todd, Reggie, Ralanda, Raymond, Roshard, Ciara, Angelica, Amanda, and Bradley you all have given me plenty of laughter, ton of experiences, and of course lots of beautiful nieces and nephews. I especially want to thank my sisters, Ciara Bender and Tamika Johnson, because, without either of you, there would be no book. Ciara, girl you are my bae forever. You had my back through this entire process. Thank you, thank you. I appreciate you more than you will ever know. Tamika, girl you were on the phone for countless hours making sure my shit sound right, listening to some of my crazy ideas, and life experiences. To my best friend Renae Gordon, thank you for being the epitome of what a true friend should be. Sereatha Berry-Virtanen, my business sister, we share this love for business that I do not think other people would ever understand. To the baddest DIVAS to ever cross the sands, DELTA SIGMA THETA, Inc. our 22 founders made me believe I too can achieve anything. Last and never least, Christopher Taylor we have been business partners for over a decade and there is no one I would have rather been in the HUSTLE trenches with but you. You saw and understood my dream, thank you.

.

Welcome!

Thank you so much and congratulations on investing in your business! That's right, no matter how small the investment, it counts and with that mindset, you and your business are off to a great start. In fact, this book was especially created for women just like you - smart and ready to allow nothing to get between you and your success!

It is designed for you to be able to read from beginning to end or for you to be able to refer to the section that you need when you need it. I sincerely pray that you enjoy "The B Book" and find it helpful to reaching your goals!

-Trenice Ezell

Section One:

Beauty

Chapter 1:

Presenting the You on the Inside

"So what your hustle offends others!
You just stay humble and approachable"
– Trenice Ezell

Let's get right to it: You are your business. We've all heard the saying, "You introduce yourself before you ever open your mouth." This is true and we will definitely spend time on why your outer appearance is so important, however, once you do open your mouth you will be doing one of two things. You are going to prove that what others initially thought of you is either right or that they were wrong. This is why it is so extremely important to spend time developing your "self". We are starting with presenting the you on the inside because absolutely everything - from the way you talk to the way that you dress - all begins with the way that you think.

It doesn't matter how great you look or how wonderful your business idea is if you are not continually growing and stretching yourself to be the best you that you can be. This involves, but is not limited to your beliefs and your attitude. Yes, I'm talking mostly about how you feel right now, and not just what you know. How you feel stems from what you believe about yourself, others and your environment. This feeling seeps into everything that you do and every single interaction that you have with others. The people around you can feel it, whether they understand it or not, and this is why how you feel can essentially affect the mood of an entire room or event. It also affects how people will feel about you and your business. I'm sure you've heard the saying, "People will forget what you did, and even what you said, but never how you made them feel." This is especially true in the business world because of competition and saturated markets. People generally do business with people that they like.

Another perk of developing yourself is maturity and understanding how to deal with others. A true sign of maturity is knowing how to keep your personal and professional life as separate as possible and having control over your emotions. Coming into contact with countless different personalities will definitely test your patience on many different levels. Spending time to develop your personal interest and inter-personal skills will always prove valuable in your business endeavors because these skills build up the person that you are, as well as what you can offer to your clients.

When setting out to further develop yourself there are many avenues that you could take. The one you chose will depend on variables such as your style of learning and your budget. There are articles, books, coaches, etc. available to you. There are tons of self-help resources that are designed specifically for whatever you feel you need to work on. As well as different personality test that can steer you in the right direction in regard to what you may need to work on. This journey will be different for each person in terms of difficulty, but it is absolutely necessary for success. So, take the time to get to know yourself and how you want to be presented to the world. Build yourself up around that image, once you have it.

B-Savvy Gems

❖ You are your business!

❖ You should always be focused on self-development.

❖ People do business with people they like.

❖ Find out which self-help resources work best for you.

Notes

Notes

Chapter 2:

Presenting the You on the Outside

"Rule number 1: Never be number 2"

-unknown author

Now moving on to your outer presentation! The gift wrapping, if I may. In the last chapter, we focused on your inner workings of becoming the type of person that you can be proud of. In this chapter we will focus on how to present this person to the world by the way you carry, dress and therefore represent yourself.

The number one message that I want to relay in this chapter is the power of individuality. You were born a complete individual with your own way of thinking and expressing yourself. Tap into that individuality and birth a style that enables you to feel your one hundred percent best.

We all know that when you look good, you feel good. We're going to take that one step further with professionalism. Dressing professionally not only lets your prospective clients know that you mean business, it helps you to remember to stay professional at all times as well. It says that you take your time seriously, as well as theirs.

A good place to start when pulling together your "look" are the basics: making sure your hair, teeth, nails and clothes are clean. Now, I know that just about all of you are aware and practice these basics. It's simply a reminder. To add to good hygiene, a healthy diet and an active lifestyle will only help in your mission of putting your best foot forward.

Moving on to making sure that clothes are the right fit, and/or are tailored to fit perfectly if need be. Finding a good, inexpensive seamstress shouldn't be hard with the internet at your fingertips and more people following their dreams. I wouldn't be surprised if someone in your circle is really good at this. Always remember to check your circle of friends and family first, since these are some of the first people you should be supporting!

While still on the subject of supporting, it's important to know that you really don't need to break the bank to look good. There are plenty of good quality, yet inexpensive brands. If labels are your style, there are still ways to achieve your looks without taping into those business funds. Gentle used stores and sites offer great opportunity to own the labels you love or the looks you're after. A little bargain hunting never hurt anyone. Having low funds is never an excuse to not look your best.

Lastly, let's talk about the extras. The lovely extras can include anything from makeup to jewelry to shoes and belts. All of these things, of course, will depend on your preference.

Again, your individuality will play a big role in setting you apart. Making sure that you are comfortable with your choices its what will help you absolutely rock your look, each and every time. If you would like to wear makeup but aren't comfortable with your skills, consider taking a make-up class. Pretty much anything you want to get better at, YouTube has a video for it. There are also some pretty cool make-up artists who offer one on one classes, as well as group classes for those who want to enhance their skills. And for those specials, moments like events or photo shoots, never underestimate the power of a professional. We are all out here trying to make our dreams come true, so whenever you have the chance and are able to support a fellow entrepreneur, you absolutely should!

Presenting your best self is definitely a process, so take your time and try to avoid becoming overwhelmed. Just think of your favorite actress or singer on the red carpet. The finished product is complete glamour. However, the process to get there takes an entire team and could take hours to complete.

B-Savvy Gems

❖ There is power in your individuality.

❖ Dressing professional sets the tone for your meetings.

❖ Start with the basics and build a look that is uniquely you.

❖ You don't have to spend a lot of money to look like you did.

❖ Being comfortable with your choices builds confidence.

❖ Learn new skills as needed.

❖ Do not underestimate the power of the professional.

❖ Trust the process.

Notes

Notes

Chapter 3:

Presenting Your Business

"Success is not final; Failure is not fatal

It is the courage to continue that counts."

- Winston Churchill

If you've ever taken a sales course, you may have heard that selling is nothing more than a transfer of emotion. This basically means that you must get the prospective client or customers to not only see the value that your product or service has, they must feel it as well. How do you get prospective clients or customers to feel awesome enough about your service or product to become a paying client or customer? Simple. You have to feel just as awesome about whatever it is that you offer to transfer that emotion over.

In other words, you need to wholeheartedly believe in your service or product. You have to believe that it will truly benefit your clients and/or customers in the way that you say it will. If you do, your job is a simple one: Allow your enthusiasm to pour through absolutely everything that you do to promote your business and get it front of as many potential purchasers as possible. If you don't, then your job is to develop your service and/ or product until you whole-hearted believe in it. This could mean anything from learning and practicing your craft more to recruiting and training the best team that you can find. Whatever it takes should be your motto when it comes to ensuring that what you offer is the best that you have. This is how you ensure that you are always enthusiastic when presenting your business.

Another aspect of representing your business is maintaining your good name and image. Even as a business owner, you are still a consumer. Right? You have good and bad experiences with those you do business within your personal and business life. How do these experiences, whether good or bad, affect the way that you do business and who you do business with? Do you continue to use a company that you have a negative experience with, whether it's the product or service, or the customer service? Probably not, right? And what are the chances of you informing anyone you know and care about in on your personal experience with this company? Pretty great, I'm sure. The same goes for a positive experience. Chances are that you will stick with the company and let all of your friends and family know what great service you got so that they can get in on the goods as well. That's how this business world works.

Coupled with the first two chapters on representing yourself, you should have a clear picture of how you want to be viewed as a business owner. With this picture in mind, you can create and build the image you wish to relay to the world about what you do. Keep in mind, not only must you create your image, but you must maintain it as well.

B-Savvy Gems

❖ Making a sale is a transfer of emotion

❖ Believing in your business 100% is the key.

❖ Maintaining your image is just as important as creating it.

Notes

Notes

Section Two:

Brains

Chapter 4:

Self-Development

"It's not just about being better. It's about being different. You need to give people a reason to choose your business."

-Tom Abbott

In our first section, we spoke of beauty, inside and out, and how you want to present yourself and your business. In this section, we will speak on the Brains behind the Beauty! Developing your "self" is really the first step behind it all. However, it is much more of a journey than a destination. Self-developing is a never-ending endeavor that should continue throughout your many transitions in business and in life. In other words, you should always be striving for growth and progress versus perfection. For simplicity, we've broken down self-development into three categories. Please keep in mind that this is a personal journey, so it will undoubtedly be different for each individual. Find routines that work for you and practice them daily.

The first category is spirituality and self-care. You already know that it is impossible to give to anyone else (family, friends, or even customers and clients) that of which you do not have yourself. You must find a balance and peace within yourself in order to present it to the world. Your religious and/or spiritual beliefs are that of your own. Find what makes sense to you, a belief that feeds your soul and stay connected to that power. You don't owe it to anyone outside of yourself to understand your beliefs, just make sure that you do. Self-care, as the name implies also extends to the things you do daily, weekly, monthly and annually to care for yourself. This can be as simply as a daily bath ritual, a weekly manicure and pedicure, a monthly massage or facial, and/or your annual exams. Putting yourself first, before your family and your business, is not selfish. It's necessary when you want to be guiding force behind both of those fulfilling endeavors.

The second category is your family and your friends. In the same sense that taking care of yourself is super important. Nurturing your relationships are just as important. Your family and your friends should be your support system. Having someone to talk to about anything that may pop up, personal or business related is a god send. Having people in your life that you can trust with anything is an absolute god send. These types of relationships just don't happen overnight. You have to nurture those relationships. You all know of the very popular saying, "the grass isn't always greener on the other side," right?? Of course you have! Well this is true and I feel that you need to understand why this is so true. It's because the grass is greener where it is watered, plain and simple. That grass may very well appear greener because it is being consistently watered by someone one. The reason it looks extra green to an outsider is because they haven't had to sacrifice and provide for said grass. Put in the work for your own pastures and then appreciate them for what they have grown to be. And it all may seem unrelated when it comes to growing your business, but it's not. Having your life together as a whole only leads to a more stable business.

Which leads us to our third category: your career, business, and finances. The first step is deciding what career path or business choice you are interested in. Most may know this already, but if not a good place to start is with your current interests, something that you've always had interest in, or maybe even volunteering within an industry that you think you might have interest in. The key word being interest! Whatever you decide to do has to be something that you are or can develop a passion for. Just consider the amount of time and effort it is going to take to manifest your endeavor. In some cases, the only thing that will propelling you forward is the love you have for your project. Without that passion, it's going to be extremely hard to continue when things get hard; and they will get hard. The second step, which will be discussed further in this section is to become completely immersed in your industry. You must become the expert in your field, and even then the learning and growing should never end. Industries change and grow, just as you are. Your job is to stay on top of that and at some point even be able to predict these changes; hence the consultant position. When you truly have a passion for your industry, this won't seem like such a daunting task, it'll be a welcomed challenge.

B-Savvy Gems

❖ Your journey is just that, yours.

❖ Nurturing your relationship with yourself and your loved ones is important.

❖ Figuring out what your interests are will lead to uncovering your passion.

Notes

Notes

Chapter 5:

Staying Knowledgeable in Your Industry

"Education changes the intellectual and moral atmosphere; it changes the thinking of a man … knowledge is the prime need of the hour."

- Mary McLeod Bethune

With a good grip on developing the different categories that make up your life, your next focus is on your industry. Like we discussed in the last chapter, you choose this industry for one of two reasons: You were good at it naturally or you worked really hard to become good at it because you developed an interest for whatever reason. Allow this attraction to guide you in learning everything you possibly can about your industry.

First of all, we now live in an age where everything is accessible. Absolutely everything. So, no matter what your schedule is like you can find a class, a seminar, a webinar, and even just a chat session that can help you stay on your learning mission. This goes double for your budget, as there are tons of free resources out there for just about every industry. This includes libraries that now offer e-books and audio books available for free that can be used on your mobile devices. This is big. It literally means that you have absolutely no excuse not to be growing and progressing each and every day. There is nothing standing in your way. Just take a moment to let that sink in.

Got it? Good. Now get to work on absorbing all that there is to know about your industry. This includes knowing your niche if you chose to have one. Knowing your demographics or territories, knowing your customers, knowing your products. It also involves knowing your competition. How else will you know and understand what makes you and your business different? You have to understand your edge in order to have one.

B-Savvy Gems

❖ Make continued learning a priority.

❖ You must be an expert in your field and there is no excuse not to be.

❖ You must understand your edge in order to have one.

Notes

Notes

Chapter 6:

The Importance of Mentorship & Experiences

"Those who bring sunshine to the lives of others cannot keep it from themselves."

- James Bame

Have you ever heard the saying, "Learning from your own mistakes is smart; Learning from someone else's mistakes is wise; not learning from either is just foolish," (author unknown)? Well, it's the absolute truth and does not only pertain to mistakes. You should be learning from other people's successes as well!

At the very least you should be out there learning and figuring out what works and what does not work for you and your business. However, if you really want to make the biggest impact in the shortest amount of time, you will find that a mentor's help is priceless. This mentor is someone who can assist you when just starting out, someone who helps you maneuver the many transitions you are bound to make throughout your journey or can be someone who you call on when you need some guidance on a particular matter. Finding someone within your industry that has grown and maintained a position similar to the one you seek is ideal, but not the only way. In some cases, the mentor may be very busy or involved in their own business. If you find yourself doing more chasing than learning, it may be more to your benefit to hire a coach or join a network such as ours: Girlfriends In Biz, LLC. Where you are guaranteed a set amount of time and/or resources to help further your progress in learning your industry with more than a few brains to pick and collaborate with.

B-Savvy Gems

❖ Learn from your own mistakes, as well as others to speed up the learning process.

❖ Having a mentor offers invaluable guidance.

Notes

Notes

Section 3:

Business

Chapter 7:

Business Basics 101

"What we have done for ourselves alone dies with us; what we have done for others and the world remains and is immortal."

-Albert Pike

Believe it or not, there are some people that only get into entrepreneurship because it looks cool or easy or a combination of both. Don't worry, I know this isn't you. I know that you take your business seriously and are more than willing to put together a foundation that your business can solidly grow from. It's a good thing, too. Because running a business, especially growing one from the ground up, is a lot of things; easy isn't one of them. And yes, it's pretty cool to be an entrepreneur, but that won't keep the checks deposited if you don't know what you're doing.

The following are a few of the basics to growing and maintaining a profitable business:

✓ Your Plan – this can be as simple as a one-page outline of who, what, when, where, and why. It can also get as complicated as a detailed 150 plus page business plan geared towards investors. Start where you are with what you have and explain (if only for yourself) what you want your business to grow into, how you plan to grow it to that, and why it is important that you do. This plan will pull together the majority of your initial research and industry learning, as you map out your mission as a company, your ideal client, and details about the product or service that you will provide.

✓ Business structure – when you are ready to make things official within your business you will need to choose a business structure. Your choices will vary depending on your type of business, but the most used choices are a proprietorship, a partnership, a limited liability corporation, or a full out incorporation. I recommend seeking the advice of a business lawyer and accountant to determine which is best for you and your business.

✓ Accounting Plan – this may be a part of your business or separate. Either way, it is extremely important to plan ahead and account for your finances for several reasons. The two most important being filing taxes and making a profit. If you do not have systems in place that assist you in tracking your finances, there will be no way of scaling your businesses for further success and ensuring that everything is as it should be.

✓ Marketing Plan – This too may be a part of your business plan or separate. And you guessed it, it's just as important! I mean, what is the point of making the best product ever or developing your skills to provide top-notch service, if no one ever knows that you exist.

How do you plan to get out in front of your clients and customers and stay there? Put it on paper so that you can test out different marketing avenues. Make adjustments where needed and get rid of what doesn't work for your business.

✓ Sales Plan – Take some time to consider how you will continue to develop your product or services to keep a steady stream of customers and clients.

✓ People Management – Have a plan for growth in place. Will you take on more employees as your client list grows? At what point will you hire an assistant? Will you make them employees or independent contractors? These questions are better answered before the need arises to keep your business flowing smoothly in the face of expansion.

In fact, having a solid understanding of each of these points will show profitable when you are able to grow and scale your business with minimal interruptions because all of the heavy thinking and planning has already been done.

B-Savvy Gems

❖ Don't be the person who doesn't take their business seriously!

❖ In order to properly grow a business, you need a plan in place.

❖ There are several layers to a good business plan.

Notes

Notes

Chapter 8:

Taking Calculated Risks

"To make a profit, stay focused and set some major ass goals."

-Trenice Ezell

Having mapped out your business plan for growth and success, it'll be easier to gauge how much of a risk you are able and willing to take in the name of progression. Risks come in different shapes and sizes. Many people think of money when thinking of risks. However, there is much more to consider. For example, your time is a resource that you cannot recoup. Your audience, your team. All resources that are just as important as money when considering what risks, you can afford to take.

Here a few tips when deciding whether or not to take on new risks:

- ✓ Learn all you can about the risk. Will the outcome be worth the potential harm it could cause? Is there a better way to go about the change that will minimize the amount of risk involved? Is this the right time or situation to implements new changes?
- ✓ Can the risk be broken down so that any potential harm is minimized? For example, can big purchases be made over time so that cash flow is not interrupted, etc?
- ✓ Can the risk be a joint venture, where a potential loss can be shared instead of being sustained as a huge blow to just one entity?

✓ Can you afford not to take this risk? In some situations, the actual risk is in staying the same. For example, will you lose current clients or customers if you don't hire an assistant (like, yesterday)??

This is just a short list, but you get the idea. Risk management is an industry within itself. That should signify its importance to maintaining a long-term business. Take your time, consider all avenues, and consult with a professional if things are still unclear.

B-Savvy Gems

- ❖ Not all risks are pertaining to money. Your most valuable asset may be your team or your audience.

- ❖ Risks should be calculated.

- ❖ Not making a timely decision is a risk within itself.

Notes

Notes

Chapter 9:

Capitalizing Relationships

"Pulling a good network together takes effort,
sincerity, and time."

- Alan Collins

Your net worth is directly proportional to your network. You know this. We all know this. The real question is how to maximize your relationships so that they are equally and fully beneficial to all parties involved. Gathering and handing out a bunch of business cards will equate to zero increase for you and your business if they sit in a pile on your desk. Or worse: end up in the trash! Make the most of your connections with the following tips.

Represent yourself and your business well. We've already touched on this but is extremely important to reiterate it here as well. You want your colleagues to be proud to be associated with you and your business. You want to be well put together and you want to deliver on whatever promises your company makes to its clients and customers. Word of mouth is arguably the most powerful marketing tool available and its free in most cases. When someone is in love with your image and the product you produce (even if you offer a service, the final outcome is your product) you can see, hear and most importantly feel their passion and approval whenever they communicate that to someone else. That is what will compel the next person to give you a chance and continue to come back.

Be kind and helpful. This should go without saying, but we will say it anyway. Being approachable will open up doors that you didn't realize you were blocking for yourself. If people don't believe that they can come to you without rejection, they may never ask you that question that could lead to your next big gig. It happens every day. Just as you will do business with people you know, like and trust. It has to feel right and sometimes you may not realize you are shutting people out. There is a difference between being a know it all and being an expert in your field. An expert realizes their knowledge, paired with other expert's knowledge and experiences are what complete the full picture for any industry. For this reason, they are always learning and sharing ideas with the other experts in their field. This is where being helpful comes into play. As you come across articles, books, experts, opportunities, and other resources that you know others will benefit from: Share it. People will come to know you as the expert. They will feel like they know you. You are giving them value so they will like you and trust you. So, when an opportunity arises and they need the absolute best person to work with, guess who will be top of mind? That's right my dear, you.

These tips will help you to interact and engage with your audience and colleagues in a way that will be rapport over time. This is how you *really* build a tribe of people who will cheer you on and support your efforts. You never know how you will impact someone and how someone can impact you.

B-Savvy Gems

❖ How you represent yourself and your business matters!

❖ Always be kind. Always be helpful.

❖ Be a true expert in your industry.

❖ Interact and engage with your audience.

Notes

Notes

Section 4:

Branding

Chapter 10:

Reinvent your F*cking Self

"The leaves are about to show us how lovely
it is to let the dead things go."

-   Unknown

In section one and two we touched on developing and presenting the "You" that you want to portray to the world. In this section, we take it a step further by keeping your audience guessing! How do you do this? By switching it up every now and then. This doesn't have to mean a complete overhaul. But it can. That's the beauty of reinventing yourself. It's still all based on you. Your Wants. Your needs. Your desire to express yourself. As you grow, your business will grow. Just as you are not the same as you were 5 years ago, last year or even last week. Neither is your business. Here are a few tips to get started with reinventing...

Focus on critique, instead of criticism. There will always be naysayers in every level of life. It can be super easy to let the opinions of others get you down or have you feeling as if you are not enough. Let me be very clear that this is not a reason to do you differently. The want or need to reinvent should come from a mindset of, "I want to be my absolute best self for MYSELF." Now with that being said, a good self-critique or a few pointers from someone who you know and feel has your best interest at heart is invaluable. Being able to isolate areas you want to work on and apply your focus will get you the results you seek quickly. Allowing anyone outside of your skin to make you feel any less of yourself is counter-productive. Take responsibility for yourself and start working on you to your liking!

Get a mentor. The truth is that you may not have all of the answers. It very possible that you are in your current state because you simply do not know any better. There is absolutely nothing wrong with that. However, there is something wrong with staying where you are because you refuse to seek help in getting to where you want to in life. Whether you are trying to achieve a certain look or gain a certain position or anything in between. Chances are that someone before has done it and learned a better way of getting to the goal. Don't be afraid to seek out that expertise. This can mean hiring someone directly to guide you or it can simply mean purchasing a book written by someone who is where you want to be. However, you decide to do it, never stop seeking the knowledge.

Lastly, assume the position. At first sight, this may look like "fake it until you make it". But, I don't want you to fake anything. I want you to wholeheartedly understand that as soon as you make up your mind that you want to be XYZ … you are XYZ. If you want to be a business owner, you go and file the proper paperwork and guess what? You are an MF business owner. Doesn't matter if you haven't made one single dollar just yet. Your whole entire being should exude business owner because that's what you are. People tend to think that they are not truly doing what they want until they are being paid for it, or until someone recognizes them for it, etc. The truth is that you are whatever you want to be the very second that you make up your mind to be that. In fact, assuming the title may very well help you to be successful in your endeavor a lot sooner. You will begin to think, act, and make decisions like the (insert your title) that you are and inadvertently begin to attract that success right on to your front door! Your dreams really do not stand a chance against you when you truly believe in yourself.

B-Savvy Gems

❖ You should want to be your best for YOU.

❖ Don't be above seeking help.

❖ Your dreams don't stand a chance against you!

Notes

Notes

Chapter 11:

Put your Money Where your Heart is

"Three things that won't add funds to your account:

Laziness, gossiping, and fear."

-   Trenice Ezell

This entire book has been me giving it to you straight and this chapter will be no different. I'm just going to throw it out there and it's up to you to catch it: Invest in your business. There is absolutely no way around it, so there is no need to sugar coat it. You must be willing to put all that you have and all that you are into realizing your dream business. Does this mean putting your very last dollar into your business? Maybe. Only you can make that call because only you know the details of your responsibilities. What I will say is that your investment does not always or only have to be monetary. Utilize all of your resources. I.E., time, people, skills and money to get the job done properly.

When you go cheap you usually end up paying twice, if not more, than what it would have originally cost had you invested properly the first time around. Notice, I said cheap and not affordable. Always do your research and make sure you are paying the best price for the best quality that you can get. Expensive does not always mean quality and with a little footwork and know how you can get awesome quality for a great price. Also, note that going cheap can cost you in money AND time and possibly your sanity if you're not careful.

Another rule of thumb is that you must be able and willing to invest in your business before you can even expect anyone else to invest in your business. The same way that word of mouth works for you, it can just as easily work against you. It's all a transfer of emotion. If you are crazy in love with your endeavor, it will show in all that you do. If you are half-assing your endeavor, it will show in all that you do. Think outside of yourself for a moment: if you had $1000 to invest in one of your friend's business which would you choose:

(A) The friend who wakes up an hour early every day to make sure she has time to focus on her business because it means that much to her.

(B) Or the friend that hasn't updated her website since last year because her job and family life have gotten in the way.

Be honest. You are going to go with the friend who seems more serious about getting their business off the ground. Even if your heart feels otherwise. The truth of the matter is that you may even forget that friend B has anything going on outside of her job and family because she doesn't talk about it ... because there is nothing to talk about.

What you also want to make sure of is that you know and understand the different options you have when thinking of resources for your business. When it comes to money, you actually have many options depending on your personal situation. There are grants, loans, angel investors, credit card, crowd-funding, etc. geared towards start-ups and businesses. When it comes to getting help to execute your ideas, there are virtual assistants, family and friends, gig boards and more that you can look into. The key here is to do your due diligence. For every problem, there is a solution. Once you have adopted this mentality there is nothing that can stand in your way to success

B-Savvy Gems

❖ Cheap is almost never the best option.

❖ You must see your value before anyone can or will.

❖ Know and understand your options.

Notes

Notes

Chapter:12

Become one with your Brand!

"To be successful, you have to have your heart in your business and your business in your heart"

- Thomas Watson

Throughout this book we've discussed the importance of presenting yourself and your business in the best possible light, staying humble and wholeheartedly believing in your business. We've talked about developing your personal and business skills, and staying up to date within your industry. We've touched on a few business basics and how to stay fresh with your audience. In this last chapter, the focus is on pulling it all together by becoming one with your brand. Think of it as a marriage! Although both entities must be happy and complete on their own, they must also merge seamlessly in order to thrive together. Are you ready to thrive? Well, let's pull it all together!

Allow who you are and your passion for your endeavor shine through. In today's markets, chances are high that there are thousands, if not millions of people doing some variation of what you do. So how do you stand out? Be yourself. No one can be you! That is how you different. No one will have the exact same values as you. No one will have the exact same principles as you. No one will have the same work ethic as you. I can go on and on, but you get the point, right? They may be similar, but it will never be the same.

Take a step back when needed. Exhaustion is real. Burn out is real. Do yourself a favor and take a break when you need to. Whether it's a step away from your desk before you proofread a post or taking a summer-long vacation with your loved-ones, a break from the norm is good for you and its good for your business. Come back well-rested and ready to meet new demands with a fresh outlook and everybody wins!

Build and nurture your relationships. Your network means absolutely nothing if it's just a pile of cards sitting on your desk that you refer to only when you need something done. Reach out and engage. Be of service, and you will see real rewards from the awesome people in your circle!

Don't be afraid to grow as a person and allow that growth to shine throughout your endeavors! Change can be awesome when done correctly and in some cases very necessary. It can also be scary and easily discourage you. Stay diligent and keep supportive people around you.

Invest, invest, invest. Invest your time, other people's time. Invest your money, and then other people's money. Invest your efforts, and then other people's efforts. Your expertise, and then other people's expertise. You get the point, right? Invest in your business all that you have to give and then get more from other people.

Lastly, under no circumstance are you to compare your progress with that of anyone else! Read that repeatedly until you understand completely. The simple truth is that you have no idea what that person has done to get to where they are … unless you ask them. If you ask them, they become a guide for you and you begin to see the work that is necessary to succeed for yourself. That's growth baby!

B-Savvy Gems

❖ Allow your personal style to shine through because that is what sets you apart from everyone else!

❖ Take breaks as needed and do not feel guilty!

❖ Do not be afraid to grow and change!

❖ Again, invest in your business!

❖ Do not compare your progress to anyone else under any circumstance!

Notes

Notes

Links & Resources

Girlfriends In Business
www.girlfriendsinbiz.org

SCORE Association
https://www.score.org/

Internal Revenue Service
https://www.irs.gov/

Small Business Administration
https://www.sba.gov/

Create A Website

- ❖ Blogger
- ❖ Weebly
- ❖ Wix
- ❖ WordPress

Project Management

- ❖ Wrike
- ❖ Trello
- ❖ Zoho
- ❖ FreedCamp

Marketing

- ❖ HubSpot
- ❖ LinkedIn

- ❖ Facebook
- ❖ Pinterest

Administrative

- ❖ Cute PDF
- ❖ Google Docs
- ❖ OpenOffice
- ❖ Primo PDF

Communication

- ❖ FaxZero
- ❖ FreeConferencecall.com
- ❖ LetterMeLater
- ❖ Hot Recorder

Design

- ❖ PicMonkey
- ❖ FontSquirrel
- ❖ Dreamstime
- ❖ Pixabay

About the Author

Trenice Ezell, the Founder and CEO of Girlfriends In Business, She is a certified business coach, business strategies and a state and government contractor. Trenice comes from humble beginnings, Born in Chicago, Illinois but raised in Miami, Florida. Born a real hustler with parents as business owners, she watched them hustle to make ends meet. With a burning desire to succeed at a young age and being a product of her environment literally, she launched her first company at fifteen years old.

At just the tender age twenty-six years old, she cashed out and sold her first company earning her six figures. She went back to college and obtained four degrees and countless certifications. With a background in both Business and Education, her educational background has allowed her the knowledge to helping to launch over one hundred brands in which succeeded in top profits.

In her book entitled "Beauty, Brains, Business & Branding" She gives entrepreneurs the brutal truth about getting into the business. It's clear, Trenice won't be slowing down anytime soon living by the motto: Let your faith and your mindset fuel your hustle

Today, Trenice is arguably one of the most powerful networking gurus in the business. She has had the privilege of working from home while being able to travel the world networking, coaching, and mentoring women to create their successful dream business. She is known as the "3030 coach" because of her unique approach that has led to over one hundred entrepreneurs accumulating positive results gaining profits in 30 minutes or in 30 day.

She is a wife, birth mother of three beautiful children, but in total, she is the mother of seven children. Trenice enjoys spending time with her family and helping women create brands that will ultimately help them live a life on their own terms. An African-American extraordinaire with a genuine love of helping women to achieve their dream business with real profits and the sole owner of one of the largest black-owned networking firm in the country. Meet your

3030 Coach, Trenice Johnson Ezell, Author, Educator, Speaker, and Hustlepreneur.